TAKE CHARGE
OF YOUR
CREDIT

A STEP-BY-STEP GUIDE TO
REPAIRING YOUR CREDIT

BY CHARLISE R. RICE

Cover designed and created with Canva
Pen name Charlise R. Rice

Author & Merch website https://www.CharliseRice.com
Professional Resource Consultant website
https://www.LisesBusiness.com

Printed in the United States of America
ISBN Book 979-8-9879207-4-9
Workbook 979-8-9879207-3-2
Book with workbook Package 979-8-9879207-5-6

TABLE OF CONTENTS

TAKING CHARGE OF YOUR CREDIT SCORE

Good credit is critical. Credit is your financial footprint. Banks won't give you a loan if you have a bad credit score. Credit card companies will reject you and insurance companies may charge you a higher rate. If you have a low credit score, the utility company may require a security deposit before they will turn anything on.

Unfortunately, it's easy to hurt your credit score. Something as simple as being late on a loan payment can do serious damage to your score. If your actions have lowered your score, you're not alone. Millions of people have experienced the same thing.

The good news is that you can repair and improve your credit score. You have probably seen advertisements for credit repair companies, but the truth is these companies can't take any actions that you can't take yourself. I advise you to try and do it on your own before you pay someone or a company.

I was once a debt collector for a couple of years. The company I once worked for certified their employees by training on the law of collection practices, from the Federal Trade Commission (FTC), Consumer Financial Protection Bureau (CFPB), Fair Credit Reporting Act (FCRA), Fair Debt Collection Practices Act (FDCPA) and more. We also had to pass extensive tests and could not work until we did. If we did not follow these practices, the company could get sued, and the employee could be liable for the consumer debt, and terminated. I became quite versed in credit literacy and stayed abreast of industry standards. I continue to share the basics of credit literacy by facilitating a workshop with my nonprofit organization, Professional Career Development Services (PCDS). Now, by popular request, I have put together a guide to help you take charge of your credit.

In this guide, you will find a step-by-step process to follow to both repair your credit and increase your overall credit score. This will also help you form discipline and ideas to create healthy financial behaviors. As my father always says, "You can't keep doing the same thing and expect different results". This book is for people who are willing to incorporate a discipline and learn something different to improve their quality of life.

This is not an overnight process. Depending on how low your score is, it can take some time to improve it. However, if you follow these steps, your score will improve. Don't get discouraged if things don't turn around right away. Keep at it because, in the end, it will be worth it. Ready to get started? Let's take charge!

UNDERSTANDING YOUR CREDIT SCORE

Before you begin to repair your credit score, it's important to understand what factors affect it. Many people don't realize that there are several specific things that affect your overall credit score. If you don't pay attention to all of them, you can unknowingly hurt your score.

For more in-depth knowledge and understanding of credit basics, sign up for my Educational Credit Literacy eLearning workshop at https://pcds.talentlms.com/catalog/info/id:128

There are two different credit scoring models known but for this guide, I will use the FICO score model. The FICO score model is used over 90% of the time to make lending or credit-worthy decisions. FICO credit scores range between 300 and 850. Your credit score represents your ability to pay, which is your financial footprint. The lower your score, the less likely it is that you will repay the funds you have borrowed or qualify for services. The higher the score, the more likely you will get approved with no issues, and lenders will be more eager to offer you the best deals.

It's important to build your credit score. If you have a low score, lenders will be very hesitant to give you money. If your score is under 580, you are considered to have "poor credit".

 Low Credit Scores Cause

-Credit/services to be denied
-Forced to pay higher deposits
-Higher interest rates
-Miss career opportunities

There are five factors that determine your score. In order of importance, they are:

1. **Payment history.** Paying bills on time is important for your overall credit score. Late payments, having accounts sent to collections agencies, or defaulting on accounts will significantly hurt you. Bankruptcy is also very damaging to your score.

2. **Credit usage/utilization**. Credit usage is how much of your available credit you have used. For example, if you have a credit card with a $10,000 limit and you have a $3,500 balance on the card, your credit utilization rate is 35%. A low credit utilization rate is better for your credit score.

3. **Credit mix.** Typically, it's better to have experience with different types of credit than with just a single category. All things being equal, a person who has managed both a home loan and a credit card will probably have a higher score than someone who has only had a credit card.

4. **Age of accounts.** Length of Credit History. Creditors like to see that you have had credit for some time, not just new accounts, so older accounts generally help raise your score.

5. **Credit inquiries.** When someone examines your credit report to determine whether to give you credit, it's called a "hard inquiry". A Hard inquiry is when a lender, credit card, or service provider issuer looks at your credit to make a lending decision. Apartment managers, financing companies, landlords, and utility companies can perform credit check that results in a hard inquiry. Hard inquiries remain on your credit report for 2 years. Try not to have too many. The rule of thumb is 2-3 hard inquiries.

FICO Scores are calculated using many different pieces of credit data in your credit report. This data is grouped into five categories: payment history (35%), amounts owed (30%), length of credit history (15%), new credit (10%) and credit mix (10%). www.myfico.com/credit-education/whats-in-your-credit-score

As you work to increase your credit score, keep these five factors in mind. Focus on the things that have the biggest impact on your score.

It's also important that you understand the different types of consumer credit available to you.

There are four types of credit:

1. Revolving credit, such as credit cards, allows you to borrow up to a certain amount every month. You are not required to pay back the full amount by the end of the month, but the longer the balance is unpaid, the more interest is added.

2. Charge cards are essentially the same as credit cards except you are required to pay the balance in full at the end of each month.

3. Service credit is when a person provides you with a specific service and then bills you after the fact. Everything from your cell phone bill to utilities is considered service credit.

- Usually, service credit does not show up on credit reports. However, if you fall behind on paying these bills, it could be reported to credit bureaus or sent to collections, which does affect your credit score.

4. Installment credit comes in the form of loans. You borrow a specified amount of money and then repay it over the life of the loan.

Now that you understand the factors and basics of what goes into your credit report, let's get started with the steps you can take to repair your credit and raise your credit score. Time to take charge!!

STEP #1
EXAMINE YOUR
CREDIT REPORT

The first step in repairing your credit is to know exactly what's on your credit report. Your credit report contains everything that affects your credit score, including all the things pulling your credit score down.

Yes, it may be painful to take a long, hard look at your credit report. You will be reminded of the financial mistakes you have made. But you can't fix things if you don't know what the problems are.

You can get a free yearly copy of your credit report from AnnualCreditReport.com.

In the United States, there are three main credit bureaus: Equifax, Experian, and TransUnion. You can purchase your credit score from the credit report from AnnualCreditReport.com. I found this fee to be between $6-$8 from each credit bureau. They may offer a deal for a credit monitoring plan.

There can be differences between the three bureaus, so it's important to get reports from all three credit bureaus.

Once you have obtained your credit report, read it closely. The report can be long and detailed, so give yourself plenty of time to go through it.

Once you have obtained your credit report, read it closely. The report can be long and detailed, so give yourself plenty of time to go through it.

On the report, you should see:

- **Personal information**: name, Social Security Number (SSN), birthdate, current/previous addresses, and employers.

- **Credit history information:** open and closed accounts, creditor names, original loan amounts, payment history, credit limits, amounts owed, credit removal dates, and more.

- **Public record data** taken from the courts, specifically including bankruptcy.

- **Hard credit inquiries** from potential creditors.

As you read your report, look for the following information:

1. Errors. Are there any accounts that don't belong to you? Are there late payments that were not actually late? Make a record of any of these errors for later follow-up.

2. Past due accounts. This includes payments that are late and accounts that have been charged off or handed over to collection agencies.

3. Current credit accounts. You're looking for any credit accounts that are either over the limit or at the maximum.

4. Dates. Dates when reported to the credit bureau each month. Also, Credit removal dates. This is the date it will fall off your credit report for good.

You're going to approach each of the above situations differently, so you may want to use different colored highlighters or pens to flag each type of scenario. In the Workbook to Take Charge of Your Credit, there is a more detailed list of what to look for when examining your credit.

Reading your credit report can be overwhelming. Depending on your financial activity, there can be a lot of information to sort through. It can also be intimidating when you see the amount of work required to repair your credit.

If you're feeling like this, **remember that you will only be taking one step at a time.** You don't have to fix everything at once. Step by step, you will progressively improve your credit score as you take the right actions. For now, just focus on highlighting all the important information.

STEP #2
DISPUTE ERRORS

The next step in repairing your credit is disputing any errors on your report. **Do you know nearly 80% of all consumer credit reports contain inaccuracies or erroneous accounts?** In a Federal Trade Commission study, one in four consumers identified errors in their reports that might affect their credit scores.

If you think that any information on the credit report is incorrect or incomplete, you have the right to dispute it.

Credit disputes can be made online, by phone, or through the mail. You will receive instructions about how to file a dispute when you order your credit report.

Errors on your credit report happen for four different reasons:

- A creditor (bank, credit card company, or other lender) made a mistake and reported a late payment or default incorrectly.
- A collection agency incorrectly reported collecting on debt that does not belong to you.
- Your identity was stolen, and new credit accounts were opened with your information.
- One of your existing accounts (like a credit card) was compromised and used by someone not authorized.

How To Dispute An Error

If there are errors on your report (not fraud), there are several ways you can dispute them.

What is the best method to file a credit dispute?

Filing online is the quickest, secure, and easiest way to do it. You can file online through each credit bureau. You will have the option to upload your evidence. I suggest you print or save the reference number for your records.

You can also file by phone by calling each of the credit bureaus. If you choose this option, please take note of the date you called, the name of the person you spoke to, and any reference or claim number.

Filing by mail has a few distinct advantages:

- You can include concrete proof along with your dispute, like a credit card statement showing that you made the payment on time.
- You have a paper record of your dispute.
- Sending a dispute letter via certified mail ties your claim to a specific date

When you file your credit dispute, be sure to include the following:

- A copy of your report (highlight the disputed item)
- Proof that supports your claim
- A concrete, explicit request that the erroneous information be either corrected or removed

Including supporting proof is important. If you don't include enough, the credit bureau may consider your claim frivolous. If that's the case, they won't investigate the disputed item and won't issue any updates to your credit report.

However, if it's determined that your dispute is appropriate, an investigation will happen. In many cases, the bureau will simply contact the creditor in question, determine if anything is incorrect, and then respond to your claim.

Alternatively, you can file disputes directly with the creditor (bank, credit card company, or another lender). They are under the same legal requirement to investigate a dispute that you might file.

Per the Fair Credit Reporting Act (FCRA), credit bureaus are required to respond within 30-45 days. If the credit reporting agency investigation reveals this is an error, they must remove the error immediately. In a 2012 Federal Trade Commission study on credit report accuracy, four out of five people who disputed an error on their credit reports had a modification made to their reports.

 Mark your calendar
If they don't respond within 30-45 days, call back to have it removed immediately.

You can find examples of dispute letters at https://www.consumerfinance.gov/ under consumer education

Check out my Dispute Letter Package which includes dispute letter templates, reference information, and 2 ebooks of advanced strategies. If you have the workbook, look for the QR Code in the Bonus Material section. https://www.lisesbusiness.com/shop

After your dispute, one of two things will happen:

1. Successful dispute. Your credit report will be updated, the other credit bureaus will be notified, and you will be issued an updated version of your credit report. Keep and file this copy for your records.

2. Unsuccessful dispute. No change will occur to your credit score and your report will note that you disputed an item. You can add a statement to your credit report that provides context for the dispute and provides clarity when future creditors review your report.

Taking Things A Step Further

If your dispute is unsuccessful, you do have one further option: file a complaint with the Consumer Financial Protection Bureau (CFPB). If you choose to file a complaint with the CFPB, provide as much information as possible, including all your correspondence with the credit bureaus.

After you file your complaint, the CFPB will work with the credit bureaus to attempt to resolve your complaint. To file your complaint, you can go to their website, write a letter, or call.

1. Website: https://www.consumerfinance.gov/
2. Main Address: PO Box 2900, Clinton, IA 52733-2900
3. Toll Free: 1-855-411-CFPB (1-855-411-2372)
4. TTY: 1-855-729-CFPB (1-855-729-2372)

The Consumer Financial Protection Bureau helps consumers by providing educational materials and accepting complaints. It supervises banks, lenders, and large non-bank entities, such as credit reporting agencies and debt collection companies. The CFPB also works to make credit card, mortgage, and other loan disclosures clearer, so consumers can understand their rights and responsibilities.

Filing credit disputes is a tedious process, but **it's necessary if you want to repair your credit.** If you don't dispute incorrect information, it will remain on your credit report and drag your score down.

Steps to Take if Your Identity Was Stolen

If you believe your identity was stolen, it's critical that you take immediate action. The longer you wait, the more fraudulent activity can take place on your account.

Follow these steps:

1. Contact each of the three credit bureaus (Equifax, Experian, and Transunion) and have them place a fraud alert on your account. Most times calling one of the credit bureaus they will place notice to the other credit bureaus. My identity was stolen. I reported it and it took about two months to get it removed from my credit report.

2. Freeze your credit reports so that potential creditors are not able to view your credit reports. This makes it more difficult for new accounts to be opened.

3. Report the theft to the FTC and local police. This creates an "Identity Theft Report" which can then be used to resolve fraudulent transactions on your credit report.

Steps to Take if an Existing Account Was Compromised

If you believe that one of your existing accounts, such as a credit card, has been accessed by unauthorized people, you should immediately contact the creditor. Usually, the creditor will immediately cancel the card, issue you a new one, and then correct your credit report with the proper information.

Remember to mark your calendar, or set a reminder to follow up on disputes if you have not heard back in the time frame allotted. **ALWAYS, keep copies of letters you send, and letters received.**

STEP #3
ADDRESS ACCOUNTS
THAT ARE PAST DUE

The biggest factor in your credit score is your payment history, making up 35%. This means that if you have multiple past-due accounts, your credit score will significantly suffer. The objective is to get all your accounts paid and current or removed.

When one of your accounts is more than 180 days past due, it's considered a charge-off. Charge-offs are bad for your credit score and you want to do whatever you can to keep them from going on your credit report. Work on paying off accounts that are past due and in danger of being charged off.

When one of your accounts is more than 180 days past due, it's considered a charge-off. Charge-offs are bad for your credit score and you want to do whatever you can to keep them from going on your credit report. Work on paying off accounts that are past due and in danger of being charged off.

The good news is that your creditor may be willing to negotiate with you. Tell them that you're very eager to avoid having the account charged off. They may be willing to dismiss some of the late fees or let you pay the balance over several payments instead of all at once.

If you have accounts that have been charged off, you're still responsible for paying them. If you don't deal with charged-off accounts, you're going to find it difficult to secure new credit, services, or a loan.

Once your charged-off account is fully paid, your credit report will show a $0 balance for that account. **However, it will still show up on your credit report for seven years.** It is possible that a creditor may be willing to settle a charge-off for less than the full amount. You will need to negotiate with the creditor to determine if this is possible.

Past Due Accounts in Collections

In addition to past due and charged-off balances, you must handle accounts that have been sent to collections. If your accounts aren't charged off, then it has been greater than 180 days and is more than likely in collections. According to the Equifax article called Debt Collection Agencies, Collection agencies are companies that purchase consumer debt and work to recover unpaid balances. Some lenders have special in-house departments dedicated while others hire third parties to handle collections on their behalf. With these accounts, you can follow the same steps as with charged-off accounts by paying off the balance or settling with the creditor for a lesser balance. Like with charge-offs, your credit report will reflect these balances for seven years.

 Before you take these steps please look at the credit removal date. If the account is going to be removed in 30-60 days, then don't bother. It is not worth the time. In my experience, if I am working on a goal within a 3-month time frame, and it is going to be removed within this time frame, I don't bother.

Before you negotiate with a debt collector, request validation! Most times if your accounts have been sold into debt collections, the record information is not with it. DO NOT ADMIT to the debt. All calls are recorded for legal purposes and quality control!!! Validation is for the collection agency to make sure that the debt belongs to you. You must request this information. Validation is for the collection agency to send you whatever records they have on the debt owed. If they don't respond in 30 days, YOU must call back to request the debt removed. They will honor it! If they sent you validation, please review the information to make sure it is your debt.

Negotiating Key Tips
- Sometimes the best time to negotiate with debt collection agencies is near the end of the month. You may get the best deal because the goal is to close the account. When I was a debt collector, we received tiered bonuses each month. You may end up with a debt collector who may need to close an account to earn a bonus and or keep their job.
- Ask how it will be reported to your credit report. Paid in full with a zero balance or Settled in full/paid-settled?
  - Paid in full means that you have paid it off entirely.
  - Settled in full with a zero balance or paid-settled has been paid for less than the entire balance. This might still have a negative effect on your credit report. I've settled accounts and my credit score went up anyhow just depends on how old the debt is.
  - Simply negotiate by paying what is best for your situation and budget.
- If you cannot pay the settlement right away, opt to pay the settlement agreement (or full balance), by making a good faith payment, and pay the rest in 2-3 payment increments.

- Hack to get your score updated sooner with a paid account. You can also try to negotiate and pay off your collection about 1-2 weeks before it is reported to the credit bureaus again. They are going to inform you it will report your paid balance to the credit bureaus in 30-45 days. Remember they still must report to the credit bureaus on the same date they've been reporting.
- Once you have negotiated, and paid off the agreed amount, **request a PAID LETTER** from the creditor. Keep this letter and file it in your records! Debts are sold and most times, debt files are even sold after being paid off. This happened to me twice. I keep all my paid letters as proof, just in case they end up on my credit report again.

When calling collection agencies

1. Give the debt collector the verification they are asking for. Your name, address, or last 4 of your social security number. They must verify who is on the phone because they are required to by law. **Every time you call, take notes.** Write down the date, time of call, debt collector's name, and what you called about.
   a. They CANNOT threaten you. They cannot say they will sue you. Unless your account is in their legal department. Trust you would have known beforehand.
2. Fair Debt Collection Practices Act (FDCPA) mandates what industry insiders call a mini-Miranda. In an initial communication with a consumer, the debt collector is required to disclose that he or she is "attempting to collect a debt and that any information obtained will be used for that purpose".

3. Most people nowadays have cellphones. However, they still can take you off their automated dialers. Request to be taken off. It's annoying when the system doesn't connect or work properly when they call. They must get permission to call you on automated dialers.

- You can send a Do Not Contact (DNC) letter. Keep a dated copy for your records. This will stop them from calling or sending collection letters. However, you are still responsible for the debt because it will still be on your credit report. Do this step with the intention of resolving the debt. You will have to contact them. They're probably going to ask to take you off DNC, but it is your right to have one-way communication. Once you pay them off, remove the DNC so that you can receive your paid-off letter.

4. If they do not do any of the three previous steps, report the collection agency to the Consumer Financial Protection Bureau (CFPB). Give CFPB PROOF: all the details with the notes you took during the call(s) and or the DNC letter you sent. The CFPB will act and may even remove the debt from your credit report.

[Your name]
[Your return address]
[Date]

[Debt collector name]
[Debt collector Address]
Re: [Account number for the debt, if you have it]

Dear [Debt collector name],

I am responding to your contact about a debt you are attempting to collect. You contacted me by *[phone/mail]*, on *[date]*. You identified the debt as *[any information they gave you about the debt].*

Please stop all communication with me and with this address about this debt.

[If you dispute the debt, include the following:] Record that I dispute having any obligation for this debt. If you forward or return this debt to another company, please indicate to them that it is disputed. If you report it to a credit bureau (or have already done so), also report that the debt is disputed.

Thank you for your cooperation.

Sincerely,

[Your name]

STEP #4
BRING DOWN
HIGH BALANCES

After your payment history, your credit utilization is the second highest factor in your overall credit score (30% of the total).

Remember, credit utilization is the percentage of available credit you have used. For example, if you have $5,000 in available credit and you have a total balance of $2,500, your credit utilization is 50%.

This means that if you have really high balances, your credit score will be brought down. If your credit cards are maxed or close to being maxed, start paying your balances down. **Ideally, your credit utilization should be at 30% or below.**

Pay your credit card balances on time, and regularly, and your issuer will likely see you as a good credit risk and increase your credit limit. Some raise credit limits after six months. However, do not start charging more. Charge something small like a Spotify subscription and pay it off every month on time. Doing so will keep your utilization lower!

Your loan balances also affect your credit score. The higher your balance, compared to the original, the more it hurts your score. If you can pay down overall balances, it will benefit you. However, credit card debt hurts you more than loan debt, so focus on paying that off first.

Which is more important, credit card balances or past-due accounts? Obviously, you don't have unlimited funds to invest in repairing your credit. You still have bills to pay and groceries to buy. So how should you prioritize your efforts?

Because your payment history is a bigger factor in your credit score, you should focus first on getting your accounts current. Once you have dealt with accounts that are past due (or close to it), you can then move on to bringing down your high credit or loan balances. Finally, deal with charged-off accounts and those sent to collections.

So, your order of action should be:

1. Past due accounts
2. High credit or loan balances
3. Charged off and collections

STEP #5
BUILD NEW CREDIT

When it comes to repairing your credit, there are two sides of the coin. On the one side, you want to eliminate as much negative information as possible. Therefore, you tackle things like past-due accounts and high credit balances.

On the other side, you also want to add positive credit data to your credit report. If you consistently do things like make on-time payments, your credit score will go up.

How do you get new credit? One simple way is to get a new credit card, make purchases, and then make payments on time.

When getting new credit, consider these important points:

1. **You absolutely MUST make your payments on time.** If you don't, you will only be hurting your credit score even further. If you don't think you can make payments on time, don't get a new credit card. Try the small subscription method mentioned at the end of Step 4: Bring Down High Balances.
2. **Avoid applying for too many credit cards at one time.** When you apply, a "hard" inquiry is made on your credit, which goes on your credit report and can pull your score down slightly.

You can build new credit by applying for a credit card from one of the major companies (Discover, American Express, Visa, Mastercard, and more).

When searching for a card, look closely at:

- **Recommended credit score.** This will help you know the odds of being approved for a particular card.
- **Annual fee.** Some cards require you to pay a fee every year.
- **Annual Percentage Rate (APR).** This is the interest you pay on purchases.

If you don't get approved by a major credit card company, you have a few other options.

You can apply for a "secured" credit card. With these cards, you must put down a security deposit that will be used if you fail to make your payments. If you faithfully make payments on time for six months or so, you're often given the option to upgrade to an unsecured card.

You also might consider getting a retail credit card, such as a Walmart, Best Buy, or Target (or another store you prefer). These cards are often easier to get than cards from large credit companies.

 *Mark your calendar or set a reminder when your credit card is due. Also, take note when the date your payment is reported to the credit bureaus. This is usually the same date your credit card statement is released. Sometimes, you may be able to send another payment in before it reports to the credit bureaus. Hence, this can increase your credit score!*

OTHER TIPS FOR BUILDING SOLID CREDIT

In addition to getting a new credit card and using it to build up your credit, there are several other specific tactics you can use to raise your credit score.

Try these strategies:

1. **Team up with someone who has good credit and a good payment history.** For example, let's say your spouse has a solid credit history and a credit card with a relatively low balance. They can add you as an authorized user to their credit card.
    i. When they do this, their available credit becomes yours and you begin to benefit when they make payments on time.
2. **Consider keeping older credit cards, even if you don't use them much anymore.** Why? Because the age of your credit history impacts your credit score by 15%. Having an older card on your credit report extends the total age of your credit.
3. **You may want to enroll in the Experian Boost program**. With this program, you connect your bank account that you use to pay your utility and cell bills to Experian. Then you highlight on-time payments you have made to these companies and these payments are added to your credit report. Once they're added, your credit score is increased.
4. **Get a secured loan, which is like a secured credit card.** Essentially, you deposit a set amount into a bank account and then can borrow against the deposited amount. When you make on-time payments, they're added to your credit report, and your score increases. **NOT A PAYDAY LOAN,** they are not secured loans.

5. **Finally, you may want to consider non-profit lending organizations.** In recent years, several organizations have been created that are designed to help people get financing and build their credit.

HEALTHY FINANCIAL BEHAVIORS

In addition to knowing how to repair and build your credit, it's also important to implement healthy financial behaviors. If you don't have healthy financial behaviors, you will end up sabotaging your efforts to repair your credit.

Keep these items in mind as you continue to build your credit score.

Debt-To-Income Ratio

Your debt-to-income (DTI) ratio is your total monthly debt divided by your gross monthly income. For example, if you have $1,000 in monthly debt and a gross monthly income of $10,000, your DTI ratio is 10%.

The lower your DTI ratio, the better.

For example, if you're applying for a mortgage, you usually need a DTI ratio of less than 43% (most lenders really want to see below 36%). Additionally, mortgage studies indicate that if you have a high DTI, you will find it more challenging to make your monthly payments.

Budgeting

A budget helps you effectively manage your finances. It helps you calculate the amount of expenses you have every month and then balance those expenses against your income.

If you don't have a budget, you may not have enough income to cover monthly credit payments.

Comparison Shopping

When trying to get credit, like an auto loan, it's important to shop around. Different lenders offer different interest rates and fees, and these can significantly affect your monthly payment.

Compare different lenders against each other and go with the ones that offer you
 the best deal.

 Be careful with credit check authorizations because they lead to a Hard Inquiry. If you don't get the approval, your credit score goes down a few points. However, if you are approved and you take the lender's approval, your score can go up 10-20+ points.

Fraud Protection

Few things can tank your credit score faster than fraud. If someone steals your identity, they can open new credit accounts in your name, all of which go on your credit report, and affect your score. If someone steals your credit card, they can rack up thousands of dollars in fraudulent purchases and then never make the payments. A fraud alert is how I found out someone opened a credit card in my name and got approved. Fraud alerts help you act fast.

It's essential that you protect yourself against fraud. Keep a close watch on your credit statements for anything that looks suspicious. If you see anything, immediately contact the credit card issuer.

Also, you may want to use an app like Credit Karma, which allows you to constantly monitor your credit report. Note that Credit Karma gives you a credit score, but they do not use the FICO score model. However, it is a good credit monitoring tool.

If you see any accounts that you don't recognize, get in touch with the credit bureaus as soon as possible.

BE PERSISTENT,
BE CONSISTENT,
BE PATIENT

Rebuilding your credit is a process that requires persistence, consistency, and patience yet creates financial discipline.

You must work persistently to dispute incorrect information, catch up on past-due accounts, pay down high credit balances, and build new credit. If you're not willing to put in the persistent work, your credit simply won't improve.

Repairing your credit also takes patience. Depending on your credit history, it can take, six months, a year, or longer. For example, how quickly you can bring past due accounts current, your credit mix, the age of your credit, and other factors will all affect the time it takes to raise your score. As you have read, part of fixing errors or requesting validation can take at least 30 calendar days. Mark your calendar. Don't be discouraged if things take longer than you expect. Keep pursuing your credit goals as you take charge of your credit. Fight for the credit you deserve.

Remember

- Mark your calendar or set a reminder for your credit report 12 months from the date you requested it. You get a free one each year.
- Also, note credit reporting dates and patterns that can help with paying on time and your budget.
- It costs nothing to dispute items on your credit report.
- Follow up on disputes, errors, or validation requests if you haven't heard back in the allotted time.
- Keep a copy of everything, and take notes.

We went over five essential steps in this guide:

1. Examine your credit report.
2. Dispute errors.
3. Address accounts that are past due.
4. Bring down high balances.
5. Build new credit.

The consistency is to review, track, and follow up if necessary.

If you follow these steps, as well as the other suggestions regarding healthy financial behaviors, you will see your credit score rise.

As your score rises, other opportunities will open to you and possibly save you some money in the long run.

Do the work and be patient as you go. Taking charge of your credit creates financial discipline and the outcome will be greater. You got this!